Workshop in a Workbook

A Resource Guide for

Business Process Improvement

"Strengthening Interdependent Work Relationships"

This **Resource Guide for Business Process Improvement** focuses on developing managers understanding of the importance of interdepartmental work process relationships. This Workshop in a Workbook is entitled "Business Process Improvement" and addresses how departments and divisions can focus on their outputs and learn how their outputs may or may not be meeting the requirements of their customers. Of key importance in this effort is the ten-step, Team Based Problem Identification and Problem Solving Process called I.D.E.A.S. which provides an organizational model for improving processes.

Business Process Improvement
www.danduffyauthor.com
©Copyright 2019

Business Process Improvement
"Strengthening Interdependent Work Relationships"

Table Of Contents

Business Process Improvement	Pg 6-7
The Customer- Supplier Chain	Pg 8
Customer Supplier Components	Pg 9
Categories of Measures in Organizations	Pg 10
The Team Mission Statement	Pg 11
The Work Improvement Process	Pg 12-13
Step #1: Identify Output	Pg 14-15
Step #2: Identify Customers and Their Requirements	Pg 16-20
Step #3: Solicit Feedback from Customer	Pg 21
Step #4: Use I.D.E.A.S. Process for Problem Identification and Problem Solving	Pg 22-24
I.D.E.A.S.: Steps and Tools...An Overview	Pg 25-27
I.D.E.A.S.: Tools and Techniques...Selection Guide	Pg 28
Step #5: Objectives of Phase I: Identify Opportunities	Pg 29
Phase I: Steps and Tools...Output Summary	Pg 30-31
Phase I: Toolbox	
Brainstorming	Pg 32
Multivoting	Pg 33
Selection Grid	Pg 34
Impact Analysis	Pg 35-36
Result of Phase I: Problem Statement	Pg 37
Phase I: Output Summary, Communication and Feedback	Pg 38

www.danduffyauthor.com
©Copyright 2019

Business Process Improvement
"Strengthening Interdependent Work Relationships"

Table Of Contents (Continued)

Step #6: Objectives of Phase II: Determine Influential Factors	Pg 39
Phase II: Steps and Tools...Output Summary	Pg 40-41
Phase II: Toolbox	
Checklist	Pg 42
Data Gathering (Sampling, Survey, Checksheet)	Pg 43-46
Fishbone Diagram	Pg 47
Pareto Diagram	Pg 48
Flowcharting	Pg 49-50
Phase II Forms for Determining Influential Factors and Collecting Data	Pg 51-52
Result of Phase II: Problem Analysis Statement	Pg 53-54
Phase II: Output Summary, Communication and Feedback	Pg 54
Step #7: Objectives of Phase III: Evaluate Alternatives	Pg 55
Phase III: Steps and Tools...Output Summary	Pg 56-57
Phase III: Toolbox	
Brainstorming (See Phase I)	
Innovation Transfer (Contingency Plan)	Pg 58-60
Cost-Benefit Analysis	Pg 61
Force-Field Analysis	Pg 62-63
Standard Operating Procedure(s) (SOP's)	Pg 64
Action Plan	Pg 65-66
Phase III Forms for Generating Promising Solutions, and Developing a Plan	Pg 67-69
Result of Phase III: Eliminate Unnecessary Steps in the Process and Implement the Solution	
Phase III: Output Summary, Communication and Feedback	Pg 70

www.danduffyauthor.com
©Copyright 2019

Business Process Improvement
"Strengthening Interdependent Work Relationships"

Table Of Contents (Continued)

Step #8: Objectives of Phase IV: Apply and Measure	Pg 71
Phase IV: Steps and Tools...Output Summary	Pg 72-73
Phase IV: Toolbox	
Building Individual Support	Pg 74
Gain Commitment/Presentation	Pg 75
Action Plan (See Phase III)	
Monitoring and Measuring	Pg 76
Basic Descriptive Charts	Pg 77-78
1. Check Sheet	Pg 79
2. Pareto Diagram	Pg 80
3. Run Chart	Pg 81
4. Histogram	Pg 82
5. Scatter Diagram	Pg 83
6. Cause & Effect Diagram	Pg 84
7. Control Chart	Pg 85-86
Phase IV Forms for Applying and Measuring	Pg 87-89
Result of Phase IV: Evaluate the Solution	
Phase IV: Output Summary, Communication and Feedback	Pg 90
Step #9: Phase V: Success and Beyond	
Phase V: Steps and Tools...Output Summary	Pg 91-92
Individual and Group Support (See Phase IV)	
Build on Support and Continue the Journey	Pg 93
Result of Phase V: Hold the Gains-Verification of the Improvement Effectiveness	
Phase V: Output Summary, Communication and Feedback	Pg 94
Step #10: Repeat Process for Next Output, Customer or Problem	
Appendix: I.D.E.A.S.: A Problem Identification and Problem Solving Process	Pg 95

www.danduffyauthor.com
©Copyright 2019

Business Process Improvement

Introduction

Within International industry today, there are a variety of "organizational transformational" initiatives which are designed to have organizations focus on both the needs of their customers and the processes within the organization which enhance Quality Customer Service and nurture life-long customer loyalty. The organizational benefits of such an approach include: expanded market share, increased productivity, customer responsiveness, and profitability. Over the years, these initiatives have become known as: "Total Quality Management"(TQM), "Continuous Quality Improvement," "Business Process Improvement," "Reengineering, "Lean Manufacturing" and "ISO 9000"...to name a few.

My perspective includes the elements of: philosophy, principles, strategies, and tools & techniques which impact "the way organizations do business." These elements provide the conceptual framework and practical application that are necessary in order to strengthen interdependent work relationships. But conceptual framework and practical application alone do not guarantee success within organizations today. Success is measured "one customer at a time," through their perceptions, as a result of their experience in being provided with products, services and information, which are provided by every interdependent department within the organization.

With the objective of "strengthening interdependent work relationships," this Business Process Improvement Resource Guide has been developed. The intent of this guide is to provide you with the necessary resources to both establish an organization-wide common problem identification and problem solving methodology and facilitate functional and cross-functional teams in their quest to improve processes, reduce waste, enhance productivity and increase the value-added features of their business to customers.

Dr. Daniel Duffy, Author

Business Process Improvement

Business Process Improvement is a method of identifying the interdependent work relationships (processes) within the organization. Once these work relationships are identified, they can be used to establish "customer/partner" requirements in order to clarify the role(s) and provide measurement for the services that each division, department, team and individual contributes to the organization.

Process Focus is the key to Continuous Improvement. In order to adequately understand this focus, the organization must think about the horizontal nature of work and processes, not the vertical nature of organizational structure.

The diagram below illustrates a "process orientation" view of how work team partnerships are established within organizations based on the interdependent nature of the work processes that each contributes.

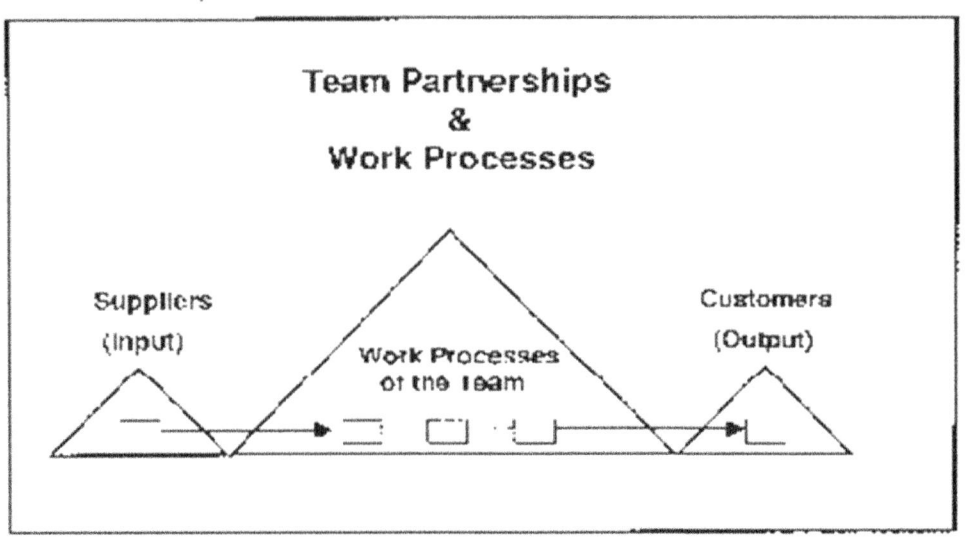

Business Process Improvement

In the diagram below, a team receives input from a supplier and delivers output to a customer. As this diagram illustrates, no team is an island, and every team works to support other teams and counts on support from supplier teams.

The three boxes within the triangle of the team represent the process the team operates to transform input into output. Every step must add value to the output. The Work Improvement Process, which will be covered in detail, will summarize the steps ranging from identifying team or department outputs to development of process measures and identification of areas for improvement.

In the diagram that follows, the individual team is shown as a link in the chain of customer value. Each team takes input and transforms that input into value-added output. Outputs are then handed off to the next team in the chain. The chain is as strong as the partnerships between teams. Every team is equally important to the satisfactory delivery of products and services.

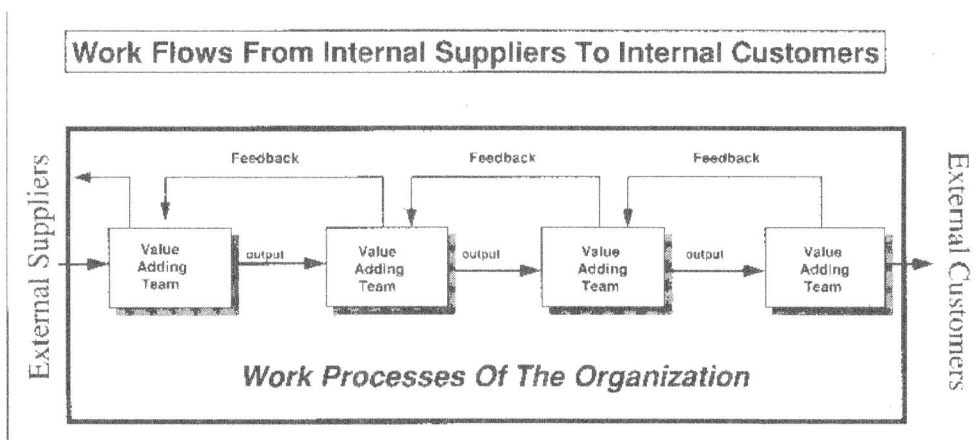

The above diagram depicts the importance of: 1.) the identification of customer requirements, 2.) the determination of effective measurement indicators and 3.) the strengthening of organization communication in the form of "feedback linkages" between and among all "value-adding teams" within the organization.

The Customer-Supplier Chain

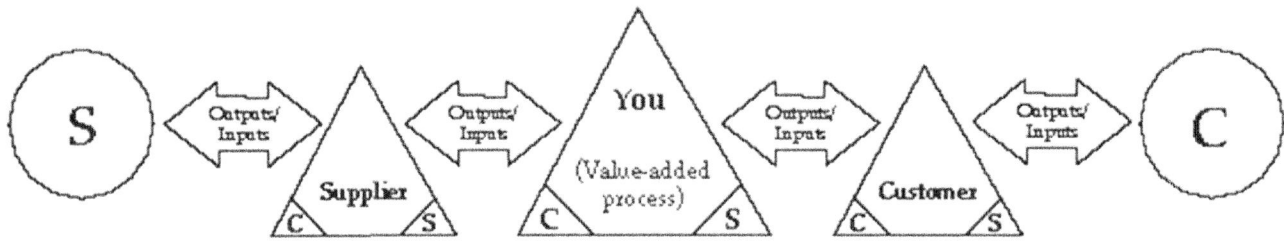

External Supplier--Internal Supplier/Customer Relationships--External Customer

> Work Processes of the Organization...
> The Key to Improvement of Our Interdependent Work Relationships.

*External Supplier: A person or company that supplies us or the organization with a service or product.

*Internal Supplier: A person or department that supplies us or our work group/department with a service or product.

*Internal Customer: An internal person or department that receives input from another internal process.

*The Internal Customer-Supplier Chain: Even though not every one deals with the external customer, everyone's job can directly impact the ultimate (external) customer, The internal customer-supplier chain is only as strong as its weakest link!

*External Customer: A person or company that pays us or our company for a service or product. ***Customer:** A customer is someone who <u>receives</u> and <u>acts on your output. Customers</u> can be internal or external. It is beneficial to consider those within the organization as both "internal partners" and "internal customers"--partners in that you need to work together with them, "customers" in that you need to focus on satisfying their needs.

The Customer-Supplier Chain

***Customer Requirements:** Customer requirements are what the customer <u>wants, needs or expects</u> of your output, ie. timeliness, accuracy, cost, completeness, quantity. The requirements should be as <u>specific</u> as possible.

***Measurements:** Measurements help you collect <u>facts</u> for making decisions. You need measurements to tell you:

1. Whether your work process is <u>capable</u> of meeting your customer's requirements.

2. How well you are <u>controlling</u> your work process.

3. Whether your output <u>meets</u> (or exceeds) your customer's requirements.

***Measurement Characteristics:** The characteristics to measure are: <u>customer satisfaction</u> (such as new and retained customers); <u>innovation (such as new products and services);</u> flexibility (such as speed of response); <u>productivity</u> (such as efficiency and unit cost); <u>business results</u> (such as attainment of financial and marketshare goals) and <u>employee satisfaction (such</u> as employee retention and employee ratings).

***Specifications:** Specifications are the important, <u>measurable aspects of your output that</u> match up with your customer requirements. Ideally, you should have a specification for each and every requirement.

***Work Process:** A work process is the sequence of activities that are carried out in performing a task.

Categories of Measures in Organizations

*Performance at the Business Unit Level: A business unit delivers a set of products and services to a variety of customers. Business units measure performance on customer goals (such as responsiveness to customer needs); marketing goals (such as growth and market penetration); financial goals (such as profit and cash flow); and human goals (such as employee skills and employee retention).

---

*Performance at the Team Level: Ideally, a team "owns" and operates a process. The characteristics of team-level performance to quantify are:

1. **Quality** (such as rework and customer satisfaction);
2. **Quantity** (such as output/input, progress on goals and amount delivered);
3. **Timeliness** (such as percent on schedule and cycle time);
4. **Use of Resources** (such as cost versus budget), and
5. **Leadership and Involvement** (such as time with customers and time in improvement of business processes).

---

*Performance at the Individual Level: The characteristics of individual performance to evaluate are:

1. **Technical Skills** (such as the level and variety of technical and business skills);
2. **Individual Effectiveness** (such as time management and fundamental skills);
3. **Individual Communication** (such as feedback, delegation, and listening skills), and
4. **Team Communication** (such as team self ratings and meeting skills).

The Team Mission Statement

In order for our interdependent work relationships to be strengthened, each functional area of the organization should develop a Team Mission Statement which serves to clarify the organizational role of the team (or department). This statement is the preliminary step in <u>The Work Improvement Process.</u>

<u>Defining the Team Mission:</u> Review the organizational principles, including values and vision/mission statements. In addition, review the organization's strategy of : Involvement, Focus on a Moving Customer, Measurement and Continuous Improvement. Based on this review, involve Associates in creating a mission statement for your team (or department) which is in alignment with all of the above.

In approaching this exercise, consider your groups answers to the following questions:

1. What is the fundamental purpose of our team or department?

2. What is the unique accomplishment our team must make in order for the organization to achieve its mission?

3. What role do we fulfill that no other team or department can fulfill?

4. What must be noteworthy about our products and/or services?

5. What will be characteristic about how we work as a team?

A good method to approach the above questions is to address them in a group meeting with answers being recorded on flipcharts. Work to craft a mission statement that reflects the groups understanding of their unique contributions to the organization.

The Work Improvement Process

Does Your Team (or Departmental) Mission Statement reflect...

a. Sufficiency: Is our total contribution to the organization's mission reflected in our team mission?

b. Boldness: Will our mission inspire this team (or department) to strive for peak performance?

c. Uniqueness: Does our mission not duplicate or conflict with our understanding of the mission of other teams (or departments)?

d. Stakeholder Buy-In: Would our stakeholders (suppliers, customers and partners) agree that this is the mission of our group?

e. Simplicity: You can read the mission to any organizational Associate and he/she will understand what we do and what we want to achieve.

f. Succinctness: Will our mission easily be remembered by the people on our team.

If Associates know what their team or department stands for, if they know what standards they are to uphold, then they are much more likely to make decisions that will support those standards. They are also more likely to feel as if they are an important part of the organization. They are motivated because life in the company has meaning for them."

The Work Improvement Process

Process Step	Question to Be Answered	Output Needed for Next Step
1. Identify Output	What is our product or service (output)?	A statement describing our output.
2. Identify Customers and their Requirements	What do our Customers Require?	A Single list of Customer Requirements.
-Identify and Prioritize Customers	Which Customer provides an opportunity for improvement?	A listing of customers; prioritized based on opportunity or problem to be resolved.
-Brainstorm Outputs Produced for that Customer	The specific Output Provided to this Customer is..?	A specific listing of Outputs for a particular Customer...
-Prioritize Outputs for that Customer	The Priority Ranking of this Output is..?	A Rank Order list of Customer Outputs.
3. Solicit Feedback from Customer	Are there any Gaps Between What I Give You and What You Need?	Completed Customer Interview Form with Nonconformances Identified.
4. Use I.D.E.A.S. Process	How can the Problem Identification and Problem Solving Process provide solutions to the problem?	The application of I.D.E.A.S. a Problem Identification and Problem Solving Methodology, to a problem.

www.danduffyauthor.com
©Copyright 2019

Step #1: Identify Output

Process Step	Question To Be Answered	Output Needed For Next Step
5. Phase I: Identify Opportunities	What is frustrating me/us the most in dealing with this customer?	Selection of an area for focusing the problem solving process.
6. Phase II: Determine Influential Factors	Does data analysis confirm that the problem exists?	List of the most influential factors
7. Phase III: Evaluate Alternatives - Eliminate Unnecessary Steps in the Process	Do we have a common understanding of the suggested solutions? Does a Standard Operating Procedure (SOP) currently exist which may address this problem (process)?	A Plan for Implementing the Solution Standard Operating Procedure (SOP) created or updated based on input from process stakeholders.
8. Phase IV: Apply and Measure	Has a monitoring and measurement plan been created which determines the extent to which the "desired state" has been achieved?	Execute the Plan and Evaluate the Solution Verification of the improvements effectiveness
9. Phase V: Success and Beyond		
10. Repeat Process for Next Output, Customer or Problem.	Has the chronic area of waste been eliminated? Has a Team Presentation been made via Storyboard to the leadership team?	

Step #1: Identify Output

Question to Be Answered: What is our product or service (output)?

Considerations: Your output is the product or service you generate as part of your job and then pass on either to the next group in the work process (internal partner/customer) or to an external customer. Ultimately, your output must help satisfy the external customers' needs.

In going through the ten steps, consider how you will plan, audit and document your progress, as well as how you will share your results with others (see Team Business Process Improvement IDEAS storyboard document).

Note that it is critical that you also proactively work with your suppliers to go through Steps #1, 2 and 3 for a sec ond time--this time with you being the customer. This will ensure that you are fully understanding both your customer's requirements and your outputs.

Activities/Questions: List possible outputs of your work group.

Use Words that:
-describe what is visible and tangible about your output;
-express what action is taken to generate the output;
-are not so general that they can describe anyone's job, but not so specific that they appear insignificant.

Examples are:
-Service A provided
-Product X produced
-Product Y sold

Step #2: Identify Customers & Their Requirements

Application: My/Our Outputs

Individual Outputs:

_____
_____
_____

Departmental Outputs:

_____
_____
_____

Output Statement:

My/our outputs provide my/our customers with (products, services) which

_____
_____
_____

These (products, services) enable my/our customers to _____

_____
_____

Output Needed Before Moving to Next Step:
   Write and Agree on the Output Statement for your work

Step #2: Identify Customers & Their Requirements

Question to Be Answered: What do our Customers Require?

Considerations: A customer is someone who receives and acts on your output. You need to understand your customers' needs by reviewing with them their requirements, ie. timeliness, accuracy, responsiveness, cost, completeness, quantity. Encourage them to be specific. Feel free to offer any technical expertise or options that you believe will improve the final product.

Activities/Questions: List your primary customers (internal and external) who receive and act on your output. If possible, identify them by name.

Interview your customers. Record, using their own words, their objectives and requirements. Try to uncover their unstated requirements. Encourage them to be specific. Ask them to classify the relative importance of each requirement using the following categories:
1. critical to the business,
2. very important,
3. somewhat important.

Remember that customer requirements are negotiable.

Consolidate all customer requirements (stated and unstated) into a single prioritized list.

Before moving on, ask:
-Do we understand how our output impacts the final (end user) customer?
-Did we write the objectives and requirements using our customers' own words?
-Are the requirements as specific as possible?
-Are the requirements consolidated into a single prioritized list?

Customer Requirements Survey
Identify and Prioritize Customers

Worksheet
Application: Identifying Customer Requirements
(Identify a list of your or your work groups major customers...)

"Who Are My/Our Primary Customers?"

Individual(s): _____

Department(s): _____

Organization(s): _____

Prioritize Customers and Select One
(Which customer provides me/us with an opportunity for improvement or a problem to resolve?)

Individual: 1.
                2.

Department: 1.
                2.

Organization: 1.
                2.

The specific output(s) provided to _____ (Customer) is/are:
1.
2.
3.
4.

Rank Order the above list based on the priority rating of your customer.

_____
_____
_____
_____

Customer Requirements Survey Interview Form

Customer: _____   Date of Interview: _____

Work Group Member: _____

What I/We Give You (Our Outputs, Your Inputs):   Priority

1. _____   [ ]
2. _____   [ ]
3. _____   [ ]
4. _____   [ ]

Are There Any Gaps Between What I/We Give You and What You Need?
(If Yes, Describe Nonconformances (measure of dissatisfaction).

Note: Numbers Refer to Outputs Listed Above   Importance

1. No _ Yes _ What? _____   [ ]
   _____

2. No _ Yes _ What? _____   [ ]
   _____

3. No _ Yes _ What? _____   [ ]
   _____

4. No _ Yes _ What? _____   [ ]
   _____

www.danduffyauthor.com
©Copyright 2019

Customer Requirements Survey Interview Form

Our work group is trying to improve the quality of the following product/service/information we provide to you (our output):

How do you use what we give you?

What are your specific requirements of us and our products/services/information?

What nonconformances (measures of dissatisfaction) do you experience and how do they affect you?

How do our nonconformances affect YOUR Customers? (What is the trickle-down or rebound effect of these nonconformances?)

Thank you for your time and cooperation.

Customer: _____   Interviewer: _____

Date of Interview: _____

Step #3: Solicit Feedback from Customer
Customer Requirements Summary

Instructions: Use the space below to summarize the customer requirement information which was gathered as a result of interviews conducted with your customers. This information will be used during the next step which is to utilize a problem identification and problem solving process.

Customer: _____

Customer Requirements	**Nonconformance**	**Priority**
(See Interview Results)	(See Interview Results)	**Ranking**

Output Needed Before Moving to Next Step:
Conduct Customer Interview to Determine Customer Requirements

Step #4: Use I.D.E.A.S Process for Problem Identification and Problem Solving

Question to Be Answered: How can the I.D.E.A.S. Problem Identification and Problem Solving Process provide solutions to the problem?

Considerations: Learning to solve problems effectively is one of the most worthwhile of Business Process Improvement activities.

Here are several characteristics of good problem solving:
- *problem solving requires patience;
- *problem solving requires discipline;
- *problem solving requires creativity;
- *problem solving must focus on work processes;
- *problem solving requires repetition;
- *problem solving requires honesty;
- *problem solving requires facts;
- *problem solving is about cause and effect;
- *problem solving requires interdepartmental effort; and
- *problem solving requires continuous learning.

The benefits of utilizing a common organization-wide problem identification and problem solving process are:

- *problems get solved permanently;
- *interdepartmental work relationships are strengthened;
- *everyone is able to "Do It Right The First Time;" and
- *communication and coordination are improved.

In the end, a good problem-identification and problem-solving system does more than just solve problems. It educates everyone in the habits of thinking and acting that allow Associates throughout the whole organization to increase their effectiveness.

I.D.E.A.S.: A Foundation for Team Based Business Process Improvement

The I.D.E.A.S. Problem Identification and Problem Solving process consists of five phases. At the conclusion of each phase is a checkpoint or a milestone which represents the completion of one phase and the beginning of another. At each phase milestone, you will identify "outputs" which are in the form of an output summary. The outputs from one phase become the inputs for the next phase. Here is a summary of the five phases and the outputs for each.

Phases	Outputs
I. Identify Opportunities (Choose a Problem)	Identify and Select a Problem (Written Description of Problem)
II. Determine Influential Factors (Learn About the Problem)	Analyze Problem and Verify Root Cause (List of the most influential factors)
III. Evaluate Alternatives (Develop Solution)	A solution for the problem (A plan for implementing the solution.)
IV. Apply and Measure (Execute and Monitor)	Evaluate Solution (Execute the plan and monitor impact.)
V. Success and Beyond	Verification of the improvement effectiveness

This system for problem identification and problem solving is summarized by the acronym I.D.E.A.S. This word represents the central theme behind every problem analysis effort—the sharing of ideas for the mutual benefit of all.

I.D.E.A.S.: A Foundation for Team Based Business Process Improvement

The problem identification and problem solving process I.D.E.A.S., works for all problems, no matter how big or small. You can compare the I.D.E.A.S. system to building a wood frame house. There are a few fundamental phases in the process. First, you have to excavate in order to lay the footings. Then you build the foundation from the solid footings. After these steps are completed, you can start to build the wooden frame of the house. The next phase is to put on a roof and the external walls. Finally, you can do the internal work of the project.

Within these phases, there's room for variation. Just as specific houses differ from each other, every problem is also unique and may require a somewhat different approach. **The five phases and their outputs are still necessary, but the specific steps followed and tools used have to be chosen to suit the situation.**

As we anticipate using the I.D.E.A.S. process, keep in mind that there's a particular series of steps for each phase that works for the majority of problems. And there are certain basic tools (like the hammer or ruler in house building) that are almost always very useful for problem solving. These steps and tools are what are presented in detail within the following pages of this Team Based Business Process Improvement Toolbox. You will find that once you've learned the steps and understand how to apply the tools, you can use them in new combinations, as required by each problem.

Following please find the steps for each phase of I.D.E.A.S., plus a "toolbox" which contains "user-friendly" instructions on how to use the tools of problem identification and problem solving. The tools are presented in the order you are likely to use them. Several of the tools are used again later in the process, just as you would use a saw or a hammer at many different stages of building a house.

Phase I: Identify Opportunities
Phase II: Determine Influential Factors
Phase III: Evaluate Alternatives
Phase IV: Apply and Measure
Phase V: Success and Beyond

www.danduffyauthor.com
©Copyright 2019

I.D.E.A.S.: Steps and Tools
An Overview

Suggested Steps	Tools

Phase I: Identify Opportunities

A. Generate and Prioritize Opportunities	Brainstorming
B. Select Opportunities	Multivoting
C. Select One Problem	Selection Grid
D. Verify Problem	Impact Analysis
Result of Phase I: Identify and Select Problem	**Problem Statement**

Phase II: Determine Influential Factors

A. Decide What You Need to Know	Checklist
B. Collect Data: Baselines and Patterns	Data Gathering
	-Sampling
	-Survey
	-Checksheet
C. Define Critical Parameters	Pareto Analysis
	Fishbone Diagram
	Flowchart
Result of Phase II: Analyze Problem and Verify Root Cause	**Problem Analysis Statement**

www.danduffyauthor.com
©Copyright 2019

I.D.E.A.S.: Steps and Tools
An Overview

Suggested Steps	Tools

Phase III: Evaluate Alternatives

A. Eliminate Unnecessary Process Steps   SOP's
                                          Flowchart (see Phase II)
B. Generate Promising Solutions   Innovation Transfer
C. Select One Solution   Cost-Benefit Analysis
D. Develop an Implementation Plan   Force-Field Analysis
                                     Action Plan

Result of Phase III: Implement Solution   **Solution for Problem and Plan for Implementation**

Phase IV: Apply and Measure

A. Gain Commitment   Building Individual Support
                     Presentation
B. Execute the Plan   Action Plan
C. Monitor the Impact   Monitoring and Measuring
D. Measure the Results   Monitoring and Measuring
                          -Basic Descriptive Charts

                          -Specifications/Control Limits

Result of Phase IV: Evaluate the Solution   **Gathering Support and Monitoring the Situation**

I.D.E.A.S.: Steps and Tools
An Overview

Suggested Steps	Tools

Phase V: Success and Beyond	
A. Build on Success	-Building Individual Support
	-Train Associates on Revised Process &/or Standards
B. Continue the Journey	-Presentation
Result of Phase V: Verification of the Improvements Effectiveness	Formalizing Support and Establishing Process Ownership Hold the Gains

How to Learn the I.D.E.A.S.

Problem Identification and Problem Solving Process

Most Associates learn the I.D.E.A.S. process the same way as you would learn to play golf or tennis--learn a little theory, but spend most of your time practicing and doing it. If you are a member of a Business Process Improvement Team, you will be meeting over a period of time to do one or more projects.

In the team, you will get an overview of the I.D.E.A.S. process. Then you will work on your project, learning the details of the steps and tools as you go along. You'll probably pay more attention to some tools than to others, depending on how much you have to use them for your immediate problem.

The key concept to understand is that "the power is in the doing." By this we mean that you will gain in your understanding of the process by applying the tools and techniques to real-time opportunities for improvement within the organization.

Tools and Techniques: Selection Guide

Tool/Technique	Identify	Determine	Evaluate	Apply	Success
Brainstorming	+	*	*	*	*
Multivoting	+	*	*	*	*
Selection Grid	+		*		
Impact Analysis	+				
Checklist		+	*	*	
Data Gathering	*	+	*	*	*
Sampling	*	+	*	*	*
Survey	+	*	*	*	
Checklist	*	+	*	*	*
Pareto Analysis		+		*	
Fishbone Diagram		+			
Flowchart		+			
Innovation Transfer				+	
Cost-Benefit Analysis			+		
Force-Field Analysis					
S.O.P.'s			+		
Action Plan			+	*	
Building Ind Support	*		+		*
Presentation	*	*	*	+	*
Monitoring	*	*		+	*
Measuring	*	*		+	*
Basic Descrip Charts	*	*		+	*
Specifications/	*	*		+	
Control Limits	*	*		+	

Key
The above guide shows some of the common uses for each of the tools and techniques. Even though the tool/technique is taught in only one phase (indicated by the "+" sign), it can be used in any of the phases indicated by the "*" sign.

Step #5: Objectives of Phase I
Identify Opportunities--Current Situation

Upon completion of this phase of the I.D.E.A.S. process, you will be able to:

1. Select a single problem that is worth working on and appropriate for your team.

2. Write a problem statement that defines:

   a. The current problem situation
   b. Its impact
   c. The desired state of affairs
   d. The impact of correcting or eliminating the problem

3. Use a method of problem identification that involves four steps:

   a. Generating a list of problems
   b. Identifying several areas to possibly work on
   c. Selecting one problem to focus on
   d. Verifying that the problem exists and defining it

4. Use the tools of brainstorming, multivoting, selection grid, and impact analysis.

Phase I Team Process

Phase I deals with the first major phase of the problem identification and problem solving process: **selecting and defining a problem to work on.** Phase I allows the team to focus on a significant problem and state it clearly. It also allows the team members to learn what is on each other's minds and establishes a cohesive attitude early in the team process.

> **Later phases of problem solving are bound to go more smoothly when the Identify Opportunities phase is completed effectively.**

I.D.E.A.S.: Current Situation
(Phase I: Identify Opportunity)

Preparation Work...Before Beginning the I.D.E.A.S. Process...

Team Information: Complete Team Project Planning and Implementation Worksheet

Reason for Improvement: Identify a theme (opportunity or problem area) and the reason for working on it. See Steps #1 to #3 (pgs 14-21) for details on how to determine what to work on.

Phase I: Process Steps and Guidelines...

"Choose a Problem or Opportunity for Improvement"

1. Generate and Prioritize Opportunities
-*Quality Tool:* Brainstorm a problem or opportunity for improvement. "What is frustrating me/us the most in dealing with this customer?" (ie. process, procedure, inter-relationships, requirements, tasks, etc.)

2. Select Opportunities
-*Quality Tool:* Multivote on the brainstormed list to narrow down the list to three problems/opportunities which are prioritized.

3. Select One Problem/Opportunity
-*Quality Tool:* Use a Selection Grid to decide what criteria are important ie.
- Is this problem/opportunity worth working on?
- Can I/we make progress on the situation?
- Is this problem appropriate for group problem solving?
- Are we the right people to work on this problem?
- Do we have control or influence over this problem?

4. Verify Problem
-*Quality Tool:* Use Impact Analysis to determine impact of problem/opportunity ie.

a. The current problem/opportunity situation
b. It's impact
c. The desired state of affairs
d. The expected impact of correcting the problem or acting on the opportunity.

Phase I: Steps and Tools

5. Result of Phase I: Identify and Select a Problem

-Quality Milestone #1: Written Statement of the specific problem or opportunity to work on.

-Quality Tool: Use <u>Problem Statement to document written problem statement</u> or opportunity.

-Is the problem stated objectively, in "as is" terms?
-Has the group described the "desired state" in measurable, observable terms?
-Does everyone in the group have a common understanding of the problem?
-Is the problem sufficiently limited in scope?
-Is the problem worth solving?
-Can the group get (or does it have) the data required to analyze the problem?
-Are there benefits to be gained by working this problem as a <u>group?</u>

Phase I: Output Summary: A checkpoint or milestone which determines exit criteria, results or outputs.

<u>a.</u> _____ Have you or your team selected a single problem/opportunity?

<u>b.</u> _____ Do you or your team agree that the problem is worth working on?

<u>c.</u> _____ Is the problem/opportunity appropriate for your team?

<u>d.</u> _____ Is your team motivated to address problem?

Phase I: Communication and Feedback Be prepared for the possibility of making a <u>presentation to the leadership team</u> in order to clarify the issue and obtain agreement and consensus on the need for investigation of this problem.

Phase I: Toolbox
Brainstorming

Brainstorming is used to help a group create as many ideas as possible in as short a time as possible to generate lists of:

*Potential Problems (Phase I)
*Topics for Data Collection (Phase II)
*Potential Solutions (Phase III)
*Items to Monitor (Phase IV)

Rules for Brainstorming

-Set a time limit, 5 to 15 minutes
(except when flowcharting a process)

-Offer ideas only when it's your turn

-Record ideas verbatim, don't interpret
(an easel and a flipchart are excellent tools to use for this purpose)

--Say "PASS" if you don't have an idea on your turn

-Never criticize, question, or praise other's brainstorming ideas

Brainstorming may be used in any step of the process, anytime you want multiple ideas and/or group energy.

Phase I: Toolbox
Multivoting

Multivoting is used, after brainstorming, to narrow down the brainstorming list to three (3) problems or solutions which are prioritized.

Use this tool when you:
  *Need to quickly process a long list of options
  *Want to assign priorities to a list of items

> Rules for Multivoting

-List and number the options under review on flipchart

-Clarify to make sure all team members understand options

-Take a first vote: Each person votes for as many options as desired, but only once per option. A simple majority keeps the item on the list. Fewer votes means an item is bracketed [...] for possible future review.

-Take a second vote: Each person votes for a number of options equal to one-half the total number of options remaining (not bracketed), again only once per option. Use the same simple majority test to keep options on the list.

-Repeat voting until the list is reduced to three to five options. Never multivote down to only one choice.

Multivoting is used when you need to quickly process a long list of options, such as that resulting from a brainstorming session.

Phase I: Toolbox
Selection Grid

A Selection Grid is a method for selecting one problem or one solution out of several possibilities. It involves deciding what criteria are important and using them as a basis for reaching an acceptable decision.

Use this tool when you:

*Want to choose a single problem from a list of problems
*Want to choose a single solution from a list of solutions

Steps for Using a Selection Grid

-Write in problems or solutions selected from the brainstorming exercise
-Brainstorm for criteria, clarify criteria and narrow down to four (4) by voting.
-Agree on scoring system (Yes-No, High-Low)
-Vote on criteria for each problem or solution

Types of Criteria

1. Worthwhile: Is the problem worth working on? This can include quality (for the customer), cost (to the organization), hassle (to those who do the work).

2. Workable: Can we make progress on the situation? This can include support (from management and others), time (for us to see the work through to completion), knowledge (about the topic), interest (in working at it).

> Selection Grid may be used any time during the process when you have to choose one problem or solution to work on.

Phase I: Toolbox
Impact Analysis

Use this page to record the problem that your team has selected, along with the selection grid you have used. This is a preliminary statement of the problem. The final statement will be developed as a result of an Impact Analysis.

Problems	Criteria				

The Problem Selected:

Phase I: Toolbox
Impact Analysis

Impact Analysis is simply discussing or sharing experience or knowledge on the subject to uncover new aspects of a problem or solution and confirming whether the problem or solution is worth working on.

Use this tool when you:

*Want to discover what impact a situation has on people and their environment

*Want to get specific stories, and other available information, such as statistics, about the situation.

Steps for Using Impact Analysis

-Ask each team member to describe, as specifically as possible, some impact of the current situation or the proposed change.

-Discuss the stories and information that have been listed.

-Based on your discussion, write a problem statement. This includes:

1. The current problem situation
2. Its impact
3. The desired state of affairs
4. (Optional) The expected impact of correcting the problem

Impact Analysis should always be used in order to confirm that all team members agree on the chosen problem or solution.

Result of Phase I: Problem Statement

The **Problem Statement** should identify the current problem and its negative impact, the desired situation and the positive impact of correcting or eliminating a problem.

Use this page to record the finished statement of your team's problem. The statement should include: 1). the current problem situation; 2). its impact; 3). the desired state of affairs; and 4). (optional) the impact of correcting or eliminating the problem.

What is the current problem situation?

What is the impact?

What is the desired state of affairs or situation?

(Optional) What is the impact of correcting or eliminating the problem?

> The Problem Statement should be written and posted to continually remind the team to focus on that specific problem during the process.

Useful Tools: Impact Analysis, Cause/Effect Diagram and Flowcharting

Phase I: Output Summary, Communication, and Feedback

Use this space for a written statement of the problem. Include a description of:
1) The current problem situation,
2) Its impact,
3) The desired state of affairs or situation, and
4) (Optional) The impact of correcting or eliminating the problem.

Check whether you have satisfied each of the Phase I EXIT criteria, results or outputs:

1. Your team has selected a single problem.

2. Your team has agreed that the problem is worth working on.

3. The problem is appropriate for your team.

4. Your team is motivated to address the problem.

> Be prepared for the possibility of having your team, or team leader, make a presentation on your team's progress to your organizational leadership team. This process allows for direct communication in order to clarify the issue and obtain agreement to go forward.

Step #6: Objectives of Phase II: Determine Influential Factors

Upon completion of this phase of the I.D.E.A.S. process, you will be able to:

1. Develop baseline measures for the extent or seriousness of a problem.

2. Determine the important contributing factors to a problem by gathering and analyzing objective data.

3. Use a method of data gathering and analysis that involves three steps:

   a. Deciding what you need to know

   b. Collecting data on baselines and patterns

   c. Determining the most influential contributing factors

4. Use the tools of Checklist, Data Gathering, Pareto Analysis, Fishbone Diagram and Flowcharting.

Phase II Team Process

Phase II deals with the second major phase of the problem identification and problem solving process: understanding the problem and its contributing factors. This procedure ensures that the solution your team chooses will really work--it will permanently eliminate all or part of the problem. Many problems are caused by underlying factors (sometimes called "root causes" that need to be changed in order to solve the problems.

Phase II: Steps and Tools and Output Summary

Suggested Steps and Guidelines...

"Learn About the Problem"

1. Decide What you Need to Know
-*Quality Tool:* Use Checklist to provide an inventory or information needed for data collection ie: What?, Where?, When?, Who?, How? and Why?

2. Collect Data: Baselines and Patterns
-*Quality Tool:* Use Data Gathering to address the question; "What might we need to measure to determine whether or not we're doing a good job?"

3. Define Critical Parameters
-*Quality Tool:* First, use Fishbone Diagram (Cause and Effect Analysis) to categorize possible causes for a problem or particular outcome.
a. The team can multivote on the Cause and Effect Diagram in order to determine critical issues.
b. The use of this tool allows the team to intelligently use data by developing consensus of the group.

-*Quality Tool:* Second, use Pareto Diagram/Analysis to determine which one or two situations account for most of your problem.

-*Quality Tool:* Third, use Flowcharting as the most important tool in a Business Process Improvement Team's toolbag. This tool helps teams to understand and improve work processes through graphically depicting the sequence of steps of a work process.

By flowcharting current processes which are under investigation, a team gains a visual understanding of the steps in a process--particularly those steps which do not "add-value" in the eyes of the customer ie: excessive "wait" time, unnecessary approval "hold" time and other time and cost deficiencies.

Phase II: Output Summary

4. Result of Phase II: Analyze Problem and Verify Root Cause
-Quality Milestone #2: Development of a written problem analysis statement which clearly identifies problem and verifies root cause.

-*Quality Tool:* Use <u>Problem Analysis Statement to document written problem analysis</u> statement.

-Does data analysis confirm that the problem exists?
-Are key causes supported by data analysis?
-Has data been displayed effectively? (ie. Storyboard Presentation)
-Have we explored helping forces as well as causes?
-Have we created a flowchart to document the "current" process?

Phase II: Output Summary: A checkpoint or milestone which determines exit criteria, results or outputs.

a. ___Do you know the current extent of the problem?
b. ___Do you understand enough about the problem and it's contributing factors to solve all or part of it for good?

Phase II: Communication and Feedback Be prepared for the possibility of making a <u>presentation to the leadership team</u> in regard to your team's problem analysis. This will allow for communication and feedback between your team and the leadership team in regard to your problem analysis and verification of the root cause.

Phase II: Checklist

A **checklist** is a list of things to be done or items to be obtained. It's used to ensure that nothing is forgotten. Checklists can be used at many points in problem solving. One of the most useful checklists is a list of data to be collected. A Checklist provides:

*An inventory of information needed for data collection.

*Organization to avoid backtracking.

Key Questions to ask within a Checklist:

What?--What does it consist of?

Where?--Where is it located?

When?--When does it occur?

Who?--Who is involved?

How?--How does it happen?

Checklists can be used at any point in the problem-solving process when you need to decide and keep track of what should be done. The above questions help to determine why something is happening.

---

www.danduffyauthor.com
©Copyright 2019

Phase II: Toolbox
Data Gathering-Sampling, Survey, Checksheet

Data Gathering is the process by which you collect factual materials that can be used as a basis for discussion or decision. Examples of data include:

*Numbers-which enable you to measure and compare (sales volume, number of returns based on type of product, etc.)

*Words-which are useful for expressing judgments, describing a sequence of actions and summarizing decisions (SOP's, minutes of meetings, reports, presentations, etc.)

*Pictures-which illustrate spatial relationships, motion, and location (video tapes, flowcharts, etc.)

Data Gathering helps to answer the question: "How often does the problem occur--both overall and in different circumstances?" There are many different techniques for collecting data. Examples of three of these techniques are Sampling, Surveys, and Checksheet which are discussed on the following pages.

Use this tool when you want to:
 *Verify whether a problem is worth your efforts
*Suggest possible causes for the problem
*Explain the problem clearly to others
*Compare costs and benefits of proposed solutions
*Monitor effectiveness of solutions and procedures

Data Gathering may be used any time you seek information
to guide you **in making decisions**

Phase II: Toolbox
Data Gathering-Sampling

Sampling is the process of selecting a small group of items or individuals that represent the whole population in which you are interested. People, objects, opinions, or anything else can be sampled. Sampling enables the team to get accurate, representative information when all items cannot be measured.

Use this tool when you want to:

*Get accurate, representative information when you can't measure all the items you want to know about.

There are three types of sampling:

*Random Sampling: Items are picked at random out of the entire population. This method is the most common and safest way to ensure a fair representation of the "big picture."

*Stratified Sampling: The population is divided into parts that are likely to differ systematically (ie. men, women). Each part is sampled separately, usually by random sampling.

*Systematic Sampling: Sampling every Xth item. May lead to error unless you know that the items are randomly mixed already.

NOTE: The smaller the sample, the less accurate it's likely to be. If it is very important that your sample be accurate, consult an expert to determine the best sampling method.

Phase II: Toolbox
Data Gathering-Survey

A **Survey** asks people for their opinions or ideas, using face-to-face interviews, paper-and-pencil questionnaires, or a combination of both.

Use this tool when you want to:

*Collect usable data about what people know, think, or feel regarding a specific issue.

Steps:

1. Decide what you want to know.
2. Develop a set of questions to get the information.
3. Do a trial run.
4. Administer the survey.

Rules for a Good Survey

*Tell people why the information is needed.
*Make the survey as brief as possible (5-10 minutes)
*Give the survey to the appropriate group of people
*Choose the right time
*Questions should be clear and answered by yes/no, multiple choice, or true and false.

Effective Surveys are both easy to administer and complete. The value of a survey is in direct proportion to it's ability to identify consistent patterns of thought and opinion within groups of individuals.

www.danduffyauthor.com
©Copyright 2019

Phase II: Toolbox
Data Gathering-Checksheet

A **Checksheet** is a data recording form that tells how many times something (an event) has happened.

Use this tool when you want to:

*Provide a clear record of gathered data
*Ensure that everyone will get comparable data

Steps:

1. Decide what data you need.
2. Design an individual checksheet form for people to use as they record these data.
3. Test the checksheet by having someone who didn't help design it actually use it.
4. Revise the checksheet as needed.
5. Design a tally checksheet to combine the results from the individual forms.

Day Event	Sun	Mon	Tues	Wed	Thurs	Fri	Sat
#1							
#2							
#3							
#4							
#5							

Checksheets display the data needed to measure performance objectively. They provide a clear record of the data gathered about a process/event.

Phase II: Toolbox
Fishbone Diagram (Cause and Effect Analysis)

The **Fishbone Diagram** shows a large number of possible causes or a problem or particular outcome. The possible causes of a problem should be dealt with one at a time in order to solve the problem permanently. Individuals and teams use this tool to generate <u>possible causes of a problem so that they</u> can then <u>select those they want to tackle in order to make a business process</u> improvement.

Use tool when you want to:
* Get the "big picture" of a problem.
*Facilitate a team's use of their personal knowledge to identify causes of the problem

Steps for Constructing a Fishbone Diagram

1. Draw the skelton of the fish.
2. Write your problem on the head of the fish.
3. Brainstorm for major causes and narrow down to four by voting or use four of the following nine categories:
    *Machines   *Materials   *Environment   *Methods
    *Procedures *Process   *People   *Price
    *Product
4. Brainstorm for subcauses or "root" causes for each major cause.
5. Vote on "root" causes to determine which one you will attack first.

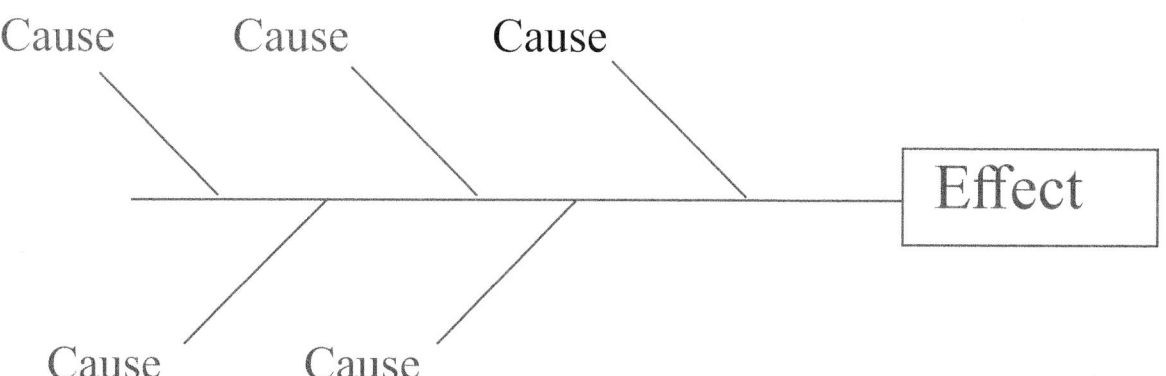

Phase II: Toolbox
Pareto Diagram

A **Pareto Diagram** is a bar chart that visually illustrates the distribution of events being studied. The most frequently occurring event is represented at the far left, with other events represented in descending order to the right. It identifies the one or two areas in which most of the problems occur.

Use this tool when you want to:

*Identify the one or two situations in which most of your problems occur.

Steps for Using a Pareto Diagram

-Define the categories to be used in your diagram.
-Sort data into the categories. Arrange the categories in descending order as defined by data.
-Make a bar graph based on data, with the highest category on the left.
-Check your diagram for a Pareto pattern (where the highest categories are responsible for most of the effects).
-Use the Pareto Diagram as a guide to action or further analysis.

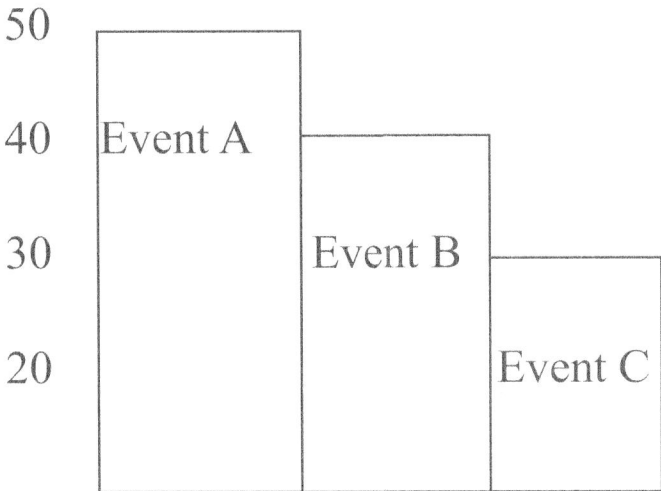

Phase II: Toolbox
Flowchart

A **Flowchart** is a drawing of the steps of a work process to show their sequence. **Flowcharting is the most important tool in a Business Process Improvement Team's toolbag.** It helps teams to understand and improve work processes by identifying inconsistencies, ambiguities, and redundancies that can be corrected on the spot.

Use this tool when you want to:

*Understand and improve the work process.
*Create a common understanding of how work should be done.

The main elements of a simple flowchart are:
>Box=Activities
>Diamond=Decision Points
>Arrow=Direction of flow from one activity to the next.

Steps to Constructing a Flowchart

1. Assemble the people who represent the various parts of the process.
2. Decide where the process begins and ends.
3. Place Post-Its on flipchart.
4. Brainstorm the steps in the process in any sequence and annotate on Post-Its.
5. Arrange those steps (Post-Its) in the order in which they occur (not the ideal way).
6. Breakdown steps to identify further processes.
7. Eliminate unnecessary steps.
8. Arrange steps the way the process should be.

> Remember that there is no time limit when brainstorming the steps in a process. You must brainstorm until <u>all</u> steps have been identified.

Phase II: Toolbox
Flowchart

Keep in mind that a flowchart can be made at any point where the process needs to be improved. It can also be used to understand a complex solution or to find points in a process where monitoring should take place.

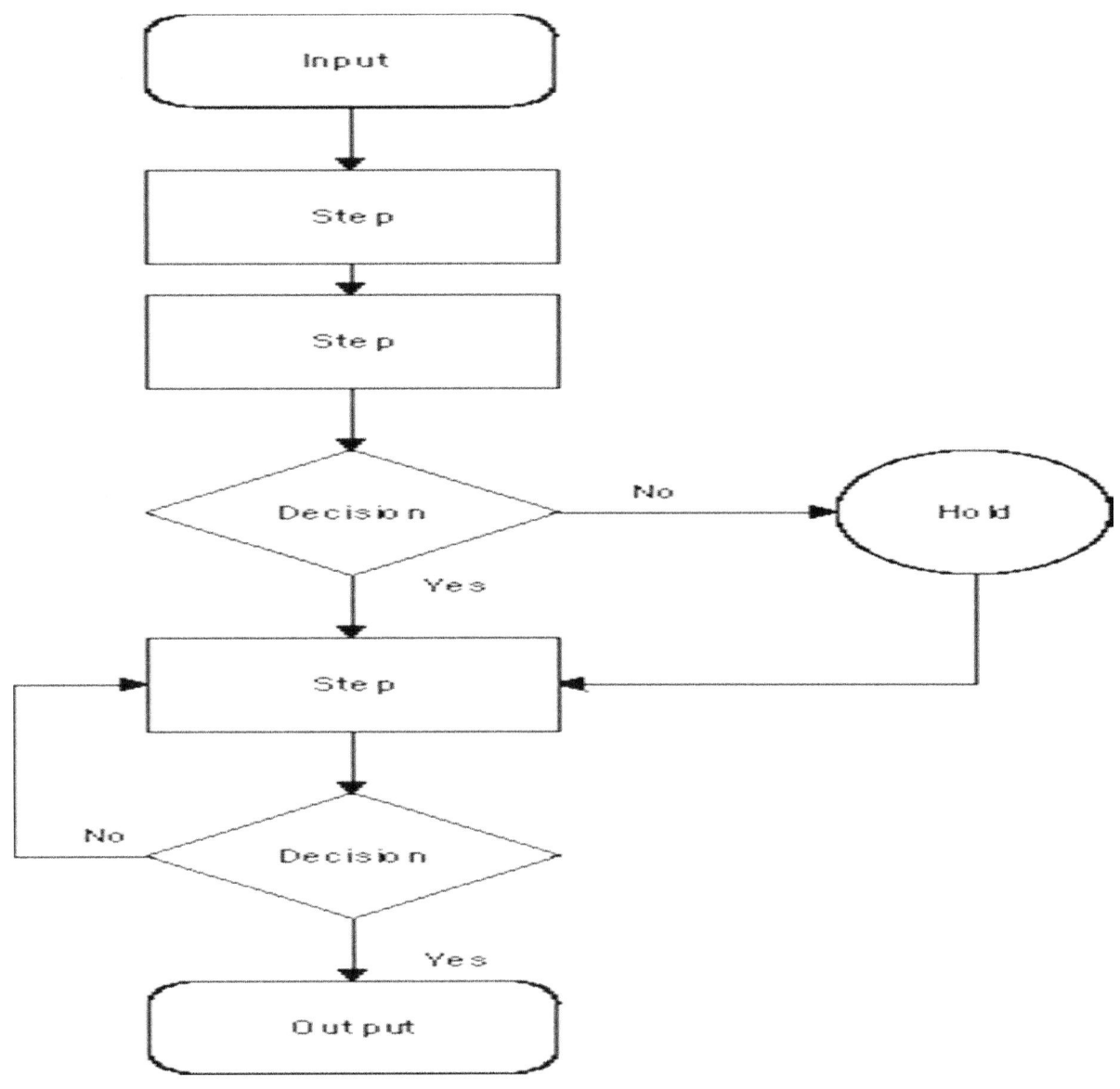

Teams can use flowcharts as the basis for designing an improved process. Flowcharts also help teams understand the current process.

Phase II: Determine Influential Factors
Forms to Collect Data:

Decide What You Need To Know

Use this page to record what data and information you need and your plan for getting it.

Date Needed:

From Where?:

Steps to Obtain...

First:

Second:

Third:

Fourth:

Who's Responsible for What?:

Collect Data:
Baselines and Patterns

Use this page to summarize the data you collect.

Your activity may include:

1. Evaluating existing data;

2. Gathering information in words, numbers, or pictures (flowcharts); and

3. Combining pieces of data on a single form. Indicate any baseline data on this sheet.

Useful Tools:
Data Gathering:
Sampling,
Survey,
Checksheet,
Flowchart,
Presentation, Monitoring and Measuring.

Phase II: Output Summary
Problem Analysis Statement
Define Critical Parameters

Use this page to record the critical parameters, most influential factors, (or "root causes") you have determined, plus any supporting information, such as Pareto Diagrams. If you are still unsure what the critical parameters are, cycle through steps associated with collecting data-baselines and pattterns.

Useful Tools: Pareto Analysis, Fishbone Diagram and Flowchart

Phase II: Output Summary
Problem Analysis Statement

Use this space for a written problem analysis statement which establishes an understanding of the problem and its contributing factors, supported with data.

1. Baseline Data:

2. List of the Critical Parameters:

3. Problem Analysis Statement:

Check whether you have satisfied each of the EXIT criteria, results or outputs, for this phase:

___ 1. You know the current extent of the problem.

___ 2. You understand enough about the problem and its contributing factors to solve all or part of it for good.

> Be prepared for the possibility of having your team, or team leader, make a presentation on your team's problem analysis to your organization's leadership team. This process allows for direct communication with your leaders in order to clarify the issue and obtain agreement on the analyis and verification of the root cause.

Step #7: Objectives of Phase III
Evaluate Alternatives

Upon completion of this phase of the I.D.E.A.S. process, you will be able to:

1. Select a solution:

    a. That will solve all or part of the problem permanently.

    b. For which the benefits will be worth the time, costs, and effort expended

    c. That can get the support needed for successful implementation

2. Create a plan for implementing the solution that includes:

    a. Necessary modifications or development of standard operating procedures

    b. An action plan for putting the solution into operation

3. Use a method for selecting a solution that involves three steps:

    a. Generating promising solutions

    b. Selecting one solution

    c. Developing an implementation plan

4. Use the tools of innovation transfer, cost-benefit analysis, force-field analysis, standard operating procedure, and action plan.

Suggested Steps in Phase III of I.D.E.A.S.

For many problems, solutions "jump out" as you study them. By the time you get to Phase III, you may have already thought about a preferred solution. Even so, the steps that follow are worthwhile. You can check whether your solution is really the best, whether it can be improved, and how you'll implement it. For more complex problems and solutions, it's even more important to follow these steps.

I.D.E.A.S.: Steps and Tools
Countermeasures (Phase III: Evaluate Alternatives)

Phase III Team Process

Phase III deals with the third major phase of the problem identification and problem solving process: evaluating alternatives which will prevent the problem from recurring, and developing a plan for implementing the solution. Phase III assumes you have already focused clearly on a problem and used objective data to understand it. Like the earlier phases, Phase III demands clear thinking and cooperative teamwork. In addition, Phase III requires you to evaluate alternative solutions that can be successfully implemented. This means knowing how to manage change in the organization by reaching understanding with and gaining support from others. Phase III also requires you to think creatively about solutions.

Suggested Steps and Guidelines...

"Determine the Optimum Solutions"

1. Generate Promising Solutions

-*Quality Tool:* Use Brainstorming technique
(see Phase I). **Options:**

-*Quality Tool:* Use Innovation Transfer if your team is in a rut. Have solutions "bubbled up" or were they readily identified? Are you having trouble identifying effective solutions? If so, use Innovation Transfer as the tool which involves using approaches from other situations to generate solutions to the chosen problem.
      a. Original Problem: b. Desired Situation: c. Related Situation:

-*Quality Tool:* Use Contingency Plan or negative brainstorming to develop innovative solutions when your team is in a rut.
a. Select Problem you would like to prevent.
b. Brainstorm actions that would cause problem to worsen/continue.
c. Prepare a Prevention Checklist/Action Plan (the opposite of the actions you have written) which will prevent the problem from continuing or worsening.

2. Select One Solution

-*Quality Tool:* Use Cost-Benefit Analysis to compare the costs and benefits, in dollars, of a variety of plans or activities.

I.D.E.A.S.: Steps and Tools
Countermeasures (Phase III: Evaluate Alternatives)

3. Develop an Implementation Plan

-Quality Tool: Use Force-Field Analysis to identify obstacles to execution of the plan. This tool will also assist in identifying action steps to reduce the strength of the obstacles.

-Quality Tool: Use an Action Plan, or an outline of who will do what, when and by what methods, when you are ready to implement a solution.

4. Result of Phase III: Eliminate Unnecessary Steps in the Process and Implement the Solution

-Quality Milestone #3: Use Solution for Problem & Plan for Implementation form to document written statement of your proposed solution.
-Have we exhausted our ideas?
-Did we avoid evaluation?
-Did we "think outside the box"?
-Do we need to get more ideas from other resources?
-Do we have a common understanding of the suggested solutions?
-Have we used the flowchart, created in Phase II, to identify where unnecessary steps may be eliminated?

5. Phase III : Output Summary:
A checkpoint or milestone which determines exit criteria, results or outputs.

a. ___ Your team has selected a solution.
b. ___ The benefits of the solution will be worth the time, costs, and efforts of implementing it.
c. ___ The solution can get needed support.
d. ___ You have an implementation plan for the solution.

Phase III: Communication and Feedback Be prepared for the possibility of making a presentation to the leadership team on your team's evaluation of alternatives phase. This will allow for communication and feedback between your team and the leadership team in order to obtain agreement on the solution for the problem and the plan for implementation.

Phase III: Toolbox
Innovation Transfer (Contingency Plan)

Innovation Transfer is used to develop innovative solutions when the team is in a rut. It involves using approaches from other situations to generate solutions to the chosen problem.

Use this tool when you want to:

*Get people out of their "ruts" of thinking
*Develop new ideas that can be applied to the problem

> Steps for Conducting Innovation Transfer

1. Visualize and describe how things would be if there were no problem. Note the difference (THE GAP) between the current situation and the ideal.

2. Think about a completely different topic or situation (perhaps outside of work) in which there's a problem that is somehow similar to yours.

3. Brainstorm a list of ways you could achieve the change you want for the new situation.

4. Based on your solutions for the new situation (step 3), brainstorm a list of innovative approaches for solving your real problem.

5. Combine, expand, and select approaches from step 4 to develop a small number of realistic strategy to apply to the real problem.

Continued

Phase III: Toolbox
Innovation Transfer (Contingency Plan)

Example:

Original Problem: Overcrowded Office

Desired Situation: More Space

Related Situation: Packing a Small Suitcase

SOLUTIONS TO THE RELATED SITUATION	**IDEAS GENERATED FOR ORIGINAL PROBLEM**
(Left Column)	**(Right Column)**
(Brainstorm this side first)	

Brainstorming is meant to be quick and fun and to produce many unusual ideas, one or two of which may bear fruit. Ten to fifteen minutes is often enough time to get "unstuck" and to produce new energy.

Phase III: Toolbox
Innovation Transfer (Contingency Plan)

The Contingency Diagram is another tool which can also be used to develop innovative solutions when the team is in a rut. It helps you to plan actions to improve your work process.

1. Select a problem you would like to prevent, and write it in the oval.

2. Brainstorm actions that would cause the problem to continue or worsen, and write those actions on the lines next to the oval.

3. Prepare a Prevention Checklist describing the actions that would prevent the problem from continuing or worsening (the opposite of the actions you have written on the lines). List these actions as specifically as possible. Negative Actions

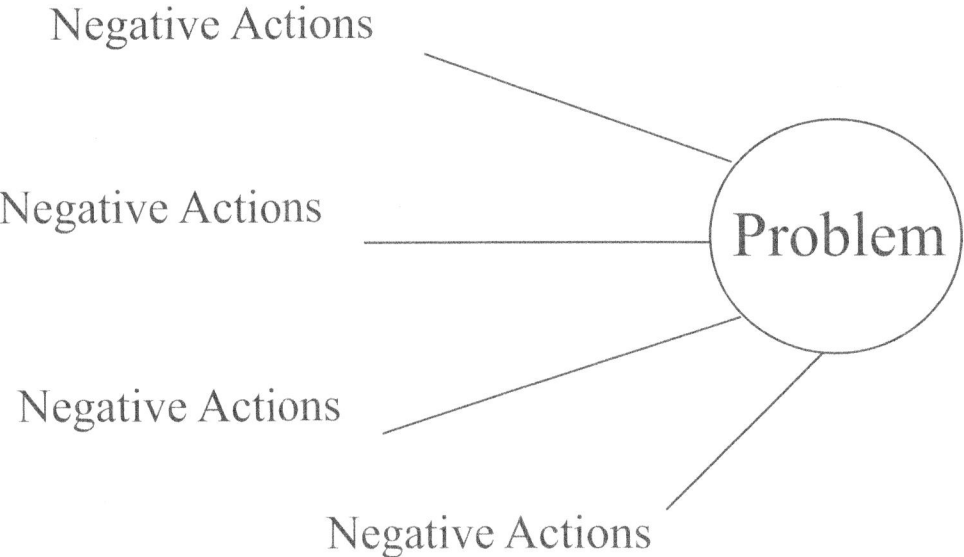

Your Prevention Checklist will become the Opposite Actions from those that you identified as Negative Actions. For each Negative Action, list the Opposite Action in it's place on the chart above.

Phase III: Toolbox
Cost-Benefit Analysis

Cost-Benefit Analysis is a way to compare the costs and benefits, in dollars, of a plan or activity. It compares the financial outcomes of different solutions and determines whether a particular solution makes sense financially.

Use this tool when you want to:
*Compare the financial outcomes of different solutions
*Determine whether a particular solution makes sense financially

> Steps to Conducting Cost-Benefit Analysis

1. Brainstorm a list of the cost factors (both obvious and non-obvious) related to the situation.

2. Determine the costs (estimate high) associated with each factor.

3. Add the total costs for the situation.

4. Determine the benefits (estimate low), in dollars, for the situation.

5. Put the total cost and benefit figures into a ratio indicating how many dollars are saved (or made) for every dollar of cost.

SITUATION

COSTS		BENEFITS
_____		_____
_____		_____
_____		_____
TOTAL COSTS	VS	TOTAL BENEFITS

Phase III: Toolbox
Force-Field Analysis

Force-Field Analysis is a method for listing, discussing, and dealing with the forces that assist or obstruct a change you want to make. The forces that push you in the direction you want to go are called "driving forces," and the forces that prevent you from going in that direction are called "restraining forces." Force-Field Analysis can identify obstacles to execution, or help you anticipate special factors to take into account as you prepare for implementation. (ie: special equipment required).

Use this tool when you want to:
*Help determine if a solution can get needed support
*Identify obstacles to execution
*Suggest action steps to reduce the strength of the obstacles

Steps to Conducting Force-Field Analysis

1. On a flipchart, draw a force-field chart (a large "T")

2. Write a problem in the box labeled Present Situation. The present situation is either the problem identified by management or the problem identified in the problem statement.

3. Write the desired situation/solution in the box labeled Desired Situation. The desired situation can be obtained by reversing the present situation or by brainstorming for desired situation/solution.

4. Brainstorm for driving forces (pushing toward the desired situation).

5. Brainstorm for restraining forces (preventing you from achieving the desired situation).

6. Determine which forces you can influence and develop an action plan to deal with each restraining force.

Phase III: Toolbox
Force-Field Analysis

Present Situation

Driving Forces--------------------><-------------Restraining Forces

> Always finish a Force-Field Analysis by making a list of action items. If restraining forces are too overwhelming, consider a different solution.

Phase III: Toolbox
Standard Operating Procedure (SOP)

A **Standard Operating Procedure (SOP)** is a set of <u>EXPLICIT</u> instructions <u>DETAILING</u> the action necessary to do things right on an ongoing basis. A SOP minimizes confusion and inefficiency, especially in new or changing processes.

Use this tool when you want to:

*Minimize confusion and inefficiency

*Create common expectations about what is to be done

*Training new workers

*Show where to take corrective action

Steps to Develop a Standard Operating Procedure (SOP)

1. Convene a group that represents the various people who will carry out the S.O.P.
2. Brainstorm all the activities (in any order) to be accomplished by the S.O.P.
3. Make a draft of the S.O.P., showing the right sequence of activities. Note who does what and when.
4. Review and refine the S.O.P., first with the whole team, then using the approval process in your organization.

Alternate Method:

1. Brainstorm the process following the steps identified in the Flowchart example.
2. Write the S.O.P. showing the right sequence and forward for organizational approval.

> SOP's should be clearly written, specific and easy to understand by everyone. SOP's should be updated on an ongoing basis.

Phase III: Toolbox
Action Plan Worksheet

An **Action Plan** is an outline of who will do what, when and by what methods, when you are ready to implement a solution. It ensures that nothing is left to chance as you set out to implement a new way of doing things.

Use this tool when you want to:

*Plan the implementation of a solution
*Coordinate data collection (in Phase II)

Steps to Create an Action Plan

1. Brainstorm what needs to be done.
2. On a chart, decide what needs to be done.
3. Decide who will do what.
4. Determine how it will be done.
5. Identify what resources will be needed.
6. Determine if there are any special circumstances or needs that should be taken into account.

WHAT	WHEN	WHO	HOW	RESOURCE NEEDED	SPECIAL NEEDS
Brainstorm what needs to be done	Date Needed	Person	By What Methods	Material Advice Equipment	Costs? Approvals?

> Always put the **Action Plan** in writing.
> You can use a Flowchart to show the sequence of activities.

Phase III: Toolbox
Action Plan Worksheet

NAME: _____

PROJECT: _____

Date to Be Completed:

Action to Be Taken:

Method(s):

People Responsible:

Resources Needed:

Special Needs:

Phase III: Evaluate Alternatives
Generate Promising Solutions Worksheet

Use this page to record solutions your group may think might work, as a result of this phase of your investigation.

Possible Solutions:

Useful Tools: Brainstorming, Innovation Transfer, Survey

Phase III: Evaluate Alternatives
Select One Solution Worksheet

Use this page to record the solution your team has selected, along with the selection grid or cost-benefit analysis you used.

Solution:

Useful Tools: Selection Grid, Cost-Benefit Analysis

Phase III: Evaluate Alternatives
Develop An Implementation Plan

Use this page to record your action plan for putting the solution into operation.

Action Plan (Attach Action Plan Worksheet):

Useful Tools:

Force-Field Analysis, Action Plan, Standard Operating Procedure

Phase III: Output Summary
Solution for Problem & Plan for Implementation

Use this space for a written statement of your proposed solution. Use the Action Plan to record your plan for implementation. Check whether you have satisfied each of the EXIT criteria, results or outputs, for this phase:

____ 1. You've selected a solution.

____ 2. The benefits of the solution will be worth the time, costs, and efforts of implementing it.

____ 3. The solution can get needed support.

____ 4. You have an implementation plan for the solution.

> Be prepared for the possibility of having your team, or team leader, make a presentation on your team's evaluation of alternatives phase to your organization's leadership team. This process allows for direct communication with your leaders in order to clarify the issue and obtain agreement on the solution for the problem and plan for implementation.

I.D.E.A.S.: Steps and Tools
Step #8: Objectives of Phase IV

Upon completion of this phase of the I.D.E.A.S. process, you will be able to:

1. Gain support for your implementation plan from both individuals and groups.

2. Execute your plan and change the work process accordingly.

3. Monitor the work process using appropriate measurement tools.

4. Use the tools of building individual support, presentation, and monitoring and measuring.

Tools Taught in this Unit

-Building Individual Support

-Presentation

-Monitoring and Measuring

-Basic Descriptive Charts

-Specifications and Control Limits

I.D.E.A.S.: Steps and Tools
(Phase IV: Apply and Measure)

Phase IV Team Process

Phase IV deals with the fourth major phase of the problem identification and problem solv ing cycle: Apply and Measure. During this phase, you will be involved with implementing your plan and monitoring how well it works. This is where you see your ideas carried into action. Even if you're not completely successful in this round of business process improve ment, you'll learn more about the situation from watching your plan at work and you'll be able to try again with greater chance of success.

Suggested Steps and Guidelines...

"Solve The Problem"

1. Gain Commitment

-*Quality Tool:* Building Individual Support is the process of talking with other individuals to let them know what's happening, get their ideas, and enlist their support.

-*Quality Tool:* Presentation means explaining your ideas to a group and getting their feedback. A presentation is more formal than building individual support but still involves two-way communication. Presentations can serve many different purposes, depending on your audience--for example, letting them know what's happening, getting their ideas, or training them in necessary skills or procedures.

2. Execute the Plan

Using the Action Plan tool from Phase III: Evaluate Alternatives, execute your plan based on project management measures such as: date to be completed, action to be taken, method(s) used, individuals responsible, resources needed and special needs.

3. Monitor the Impact

-*Quality Tool:* Use Monitoring and Measuring techniques to see how closely a situation corresponds to what you want or need. Monitoring and Measuring tools can also be useful as part of your presentation within the Team Quality Improvement Storyboard.

Phase IV: Toolbox
Gain Commitment (Building Individual Support)
Phase IV: Output Summary

4. Measure the Results

-Quality Tool(s): Use Basic Descriptive Charts (The Seven "Original" Quality Tools) to "show the facts" by analyzing data in a graphic and visual manner. These Basic Descriptive Charts are listed as follows and will be explained on additional pages in detail:

1. Check Sheet
2. Pareto Diagram
3. Run Chart
4. Histogram
5. Scatter Diagram
6. Cause & Effect Diagram
7. Control Chart

5. Result of Phase IV: Evaluate Solution

Has a monitoring and measurement plan been created which determines the extent to which the "desired state" has been achieved?

-Did we collect data according to our plan?

-Did we compare with "desired state" from Phase I: Identify and Select a Problem?

-Did we compare with data collected to analyze problem from Phase II: Analyze Problem and Verify Root Cause?

6. Phase IV: Output Summary
A check point or milestone which determines exit criteria, results or outputs.

a. ___ All relevant individuals and groups are informed of your solution and committed to supporting it.
b. ___ The plan for change is fully executed.
c. ___ Indicators are checked regularly to determine how much improvement has occurred and to spot any new problems.

Phase IV: Communication and Feedback Be prepared to make a presentation to the leadership team on your team's evaluation of execution, measurement and monitoring components of the problem identification and problem solving process. This will allow for communication and feedback between your team and the leadership team in order to obtain agreement on the assessment of the team's effort.

Phase IV: Toolbox
Gain Commitment (Building Individual Support)

Building Individual Support reinforces the importance of effective communication with other individuals to inform them and gain their commitment. It is often used before a formal presentation. Building individual support is a two-way process: you may find yourself influenced by the ideas of others at the same time that they are influenced by you.

Use this approach when you want to:
*Strengthen communication channels among associates

*Gain support for your proposal, concept or solution, prior to formal presentation.

Steps for Building Individual Support

1. Brainstorm who you need to talk to.

2. Identify what you need from them.

3. Assign responsibilities for communication.

4. Communicate to gain input and commitment.

5. Evaluate results and follow up as needed.

Building Individual Support is essentially an approach to building personal and professional relationships. The concept is built on genuine respect for others, appreciation of individual diversity, and the consistent need for nurturing two-way communication among people.

Phase IV: Toolbox
Gain Commitment (Presentation)

A presentation is a method of formal communication, usually conducted for groups. Presentation can be used to:

*Share ideas and findings,
*Gain commitment and support,
*Get ideas from others,
*Create consensus among individuals, and
*Teach skills and procedures.

> Rules for a Good Presentation

*Be clear on your goal(s)

*Keep each part of the presentation interesting, brief, and to-the-point.

*Use the Three-Tell Method:

-Tell them what you are going to tell them
-Tell them
-Tell them what you told them

*Target your content and style to your audience

*Be flexible enough to respond to audience needs

Formal oral presentations may or may not be required. Find out whether an oral presentation is preferred over written correspondence.

Phase IV: Toolbox
(Monitor The Impact (Monitoring and Measuring)

Monitoring means keeping track of how close or far we are from where we want to be. Monitoring can be used for:

*Completing the problem-solving cycle
*Identifying unwanted variation to start the problem-solving cycle

Steps for Monitoring

1. Decide what to monitor
2. Decide who will monitor
3. Plan when to monitor
4. Decide how to record and present results

Measuring is the means of obtaining data for monitoring or for any other purpose. Measuring can be used for:

*Monitoring a work process
*Gathering data to understand a problem

Steps for Measuring

1. Measure factors that you expect to be important.
2. Use only a few measures that are easy to monitor and that lead to action
3. Select measures that team members understand clearly.
4. Collect new types of data as the need arises.

Remember: If it can't be measured...it can't be managed.

Phase IV: Toolbox
Measure the Results (Basic Descriptive Charts)

Using **Basic Descriptive Charts** are a way to describe what is happening by summarizing quantities of data in simple visual displays.

Why collect and measure data?
- To reveal a problem
- To verify the existence of a problem
- To analyze a problem
- To prevent a problem

Data Collection Guidelines
- Have a clear definition of the problem
- Define precisely what is to be measured
- Carefully select the right measurement technique
- Construct appropriate forms
- Assign responsibility for the data collection
- Arrange sampling method

Remember, basic descriptive charts are Communication Devices that Tell and Show:
1. What the significant issues are
2. What to concentrate on
3. What is happening (trends)
4. If a problem is getting fixed
5. When a problem is fixed

The following Charts will be presented: Check sheet, Pareto Diagram, Run Chart, Histogram, Scatter Diagram, Cause & Effect Diagram and Control Chart

Phase IV: Toolbox
Measure the Results (Basic Descriptive Charts)

Types of Basic Descriptive Charts

TOOLS	PURPOSE	QUESTIONS
Check Sheet	A check sheet starts the process of translating opinions into facts.	How often do certain things happen?
Pareto Diagram	Is a vertical bar graph that identifies what occurs more.	What occurs most? What are the vital few? What is the rank order?
Run Chart	Displays trends over time.	Is there a pattern or cycle over time?
Histogram	Displays the pattern and variation.	What is the amount of variation the process has within it?
Scatter Diagram	Compares cause & effect relationship between two variables.	Does a correlation exist between one variable and another?
Cause & Effect Diagram	Represents the relationship between some effect and all possible causes influencing it.	What causes an effect? Why? Why? Why? Why? Why?

Control Charts A control chart is a run chart which shows if the process is in control or not.

Phase IV: Toolbox
Measure the Results (Basic Descriptive Charts)

Check Sheets are simply an easy to understand form used to answer the question, "How often are certain things happening?" It starts the process of translating "opinions" into "facts".

> Constructing a Check Sheet involves the following steps:

1. Agree as to exactly what event is being observed. Everyone has to be looking at the same thing.
2. Decide on the time period during which data will be collected. This could range from hours to weeks.
3. Design a form that is clear and easy to use making sure that all columns are clearly labeled and that there is enough space to enter the data.
4. Collect the data consistently and honestly. Make sure there is time allowed for this data gathering task.

Why use it?

To allow a team to systematically record and compile data from historical sources, or observations as they happen, so that patterns and trends can be clearly detected and shown.

Within the appendix of this resource guide is a copy of a Technical Support Team's "Customer Problem Sheet", which is essentially a check sheet that allows support technicians to capture the category and number of questions that they respond to during any given period.

Check Sheet is the logical point to start in most problem solving cycles because it allows you to gather data based on sample observations in order to begin to detect patterns.

Phase IV: Toolbox
Measure the Results (Basic Descriptive Charts)

A **Pareto Diagram** is a special form of vertical bar graph which helps us to determine which problems to solve in what order. Doing a Pareto Chart based upon either Check Sheets or other forms of data collection helps us direct our attention and efforts to the truly important problems. We will generally gain more by working on the tallest bar than tackling the smaller bars. This is another way of saying that we should focus on "the vital few" factors, as opposed to "the trivial many." (See page 48 of this resource guide for additional info on the Pareto Diagram.)

> Constructing a Pareto Chart involves the following steps:

1. Design a bar chart with the causes listed across the horizontal axis.
2. The left vertical axis should be scaled with frequency of occurrence and the right axis should be scaled with the corresponding percent.
3. Chart the data with highest incidence on the left and lowest incidence on the right.
4. Draw a line graph beginning at the top of the highest bar to demonstrate the cumulative percent impact of the causes. This line graph often verifies precisely Pareto's principle which is that 80% of the problem is caused by 20% of the causes.
5. Pareto thinking can be applied to any complex situation where many factors contribute to a problem.

> **Pareto Diagrams** allow a team to focus efforts on the problems that offer the greatest potential for improvement by showing their relative frequency or size in a descending bar graph.

Phase IV: Toolbox
Measure the Results (Basic Descriptive Charts)

A **Run Chart** is employed to visually represent data. They are used to monitor a process to see whether or not the long range average is changing. A Run Chart is used to monitor the performance of one or more processes over time to detect trends, shifts or cycles.

Constructing a Run Chart involves the following steps:

1. Decide on the process performance measure
2. Gather data
3. Create a graph with a vertical line (y axis) and a horizontal line (x axis).
4. Plot the data
5. Interpret the Chart

A Run Chart should help managers and others to think about the sytem and constantly ask themselves the following questions:

*What is going on?
*Do I like the current level? If not, what should be done?
*Are things getting better?
*Has anything changed?
*Do I like the change?
*Is the change what I tried to do? Is it in the right direction?
*Are there any trends showing up? Are they what I expected?
*Is the variation I see random or non-random?
*Should I translate this run chart into a statistical control chart?

A **Run Chart** allows a team to study observed data (a performance measure of a process) for trends/patterns over a specific period of time.

Phase IV: Toolbox
Measure the Results (Basic Descriptive Charts)

A **Histogram** is a bar chart that shows the distribution of measurements or values according to the frequency with which they occur. Whereas the Pareto Chart only deals with characteristics of a product or service. A Histogram takes measurement data, such as types of technical questions asked by Sales Associates and displays their distribution. This is critical since we know that all repeated events will produce results that vary over time. A Histogram reveals the amount of variation that any process has within it.

> Constructing a Histogram involves the following steps:

1. Decide on the process measure.
2. Gather data
3. Prepare a frequency table from the data.
4. Draw a Histogram from the frequency table
5. Interpret the Histogram

Why use it?

A Histogram allows teams to summarize data from a process that have been collected over a period of time, and graphically present its frequency distribution in bar form.

> A **Histogram** is useful to a team when it wants to discover and display the distribution of data by bar graphing the number of units in each category.

Phase IV: Toolbox
Measure the Results (Basic Descriptive Charts)

A **Scatter Diagram** is used to study the possible relationship between one variable and another. The Scatter Diagram is used to test for possible cause and effect relationshps. It cannot prove that one variable causes the other, but it does make it clear whether a relationship exists and the strength of that relationship.

A Scatter Diagram is set up whereby the horizontal axis (x-axis) represents the measurement values of one variable, and the vertical axis (y-axis) represents the measurements of the second variable.

Why use it?

A Scatter Diagram is useful to a team when it needs to display what happens to one variable when another variable changes in order to test a theory that the two variables are related.

> The Scatter Diagram does not predict cause and effect relationships. It only shows the strength of the relationship between two variables. The stronger the relationship, the greater the likelihood that change in one variable will affect change in another variable.

Phase IV: Toolbox
Measure the Results (Basic Descriptive Charts)

The **Cause & Effect Diagram** was developed to represent the relationship between some "effect" and all the possible "causes" influencing it. The effect or problem is stated on the right side of the chart and the major influences or "causes" are listed to the left. (See page 48 of resource guide under heading Fishbone Diagram (Cause and Effect Analysis).

Cause & Effect Diagrams are drawn to clearly illustrate the various causes affecting a process by sorting out and relating the causes. For every effect there are likely to be several major categories of causes. The major causes might be summarized under four categories referred to as the 4M's: Manpower, Machines, Methods and Materials. Other headings or causes are found within the areas of: Environment, Procedures, Process, People, Price and Product.

Cause & Effect Diagrams enable a team to focus on the content of the problem, not on the history of the problem or differing personal interests of team members. They also create a snapshot of the collective knowledge and consensus of a team around a problem. This builds support for the resulting solutions. Finally, they allow the team to focus on causes, not symptoms.

A **Cause & Effect Diagram** is useful when your team has to identify, explore and display the possible causes of a specific problem or condition.

Phase IV: Toolbox
Measure the Results (Basic Descriptive Charts)

A **Control Chart** is simply a run chart with statistically determined upper (Upper Control Limit) and possibly lower (Lower control Limit) lines drawn on either side of the process average.

Teams use a Control Chart to monitor, control and improve process performance over time by studying variation and its source. They focus attention on detecting and monitoring process variation over time. In addition, they distinguish special from common causes of variation, as a guide to local or management action.

> Constructing a Control Chart involves the following steps:

1. Select the process to be charted
2. Determine sampling method and plan
3. Initiate data collection
4. Calculate the appropriate statistics
5. Calculate the control limits
6. Construct the Control Chart(s)
7. Interpret the Control Chart(s)

> Teams use **Control Charts** when they need to discover how much variability in a process is due to random variation and how much is due to unique events/individual actions in order to determine whether a process is in statistical control.

Phase IV: Apply and Measure
Measure the Results (Specifications/Control Limits)

Specifications and control limits indicate what level of performance you want or need. Specifications can be used to provide a quick way of knowing if your process is behaving as it should. Specifications are calculated based on what is required by you, by the customer, or by the process.

Control Limits indicate how the process usually performs. Control Limits can be used to provide a quick way of knowing if your process is doing something unusual (is "out of control"). Control limits are calculated using the past history of the process and applying mathematical formulas. It may be necessary to obtain the services of a statistical "expert" to determine correct formula for control limits of the process being investigated.

Statistical Process Control is a method of quality control which employs statistical methods to monitor and control a process. The result is that the process operates efficiently, producing more specification conforming products with less waste.

There are a variety of industry specific **Statistical Process Control** software products which permit the organization to establish specifications and control limits and allow front-line employees to monitor production outputs to ensure Quality results.

This process relates to the adage "if it can't be measured, it can't be managed."

Phase IV: Apply and Measure
Measure the Results (Specifications/Control Limits)

Use this page to keep track of key individuals or groups you contact before or during implementation of your plan. Record any significant events, inputs, or alterations in your plan as you meet with these individuals.

Individual or Groups Involved	By Whom? When?	Remarks

Useful Tools: Building Individual Support, Presentation

www.danduffyauthor.com
©Copyright 2019

Phase IV: Apply and Measure
Monitor the Impact/Measure the Results

Use this page to record any significant events or alterations you introduce as you execute your plan.

Phase IV: Apply and Measure
Monitor the Impact/Measure the Results

Use this page to record the results of your monitoring.

RESULTS:

Be observant of any **Emerging New Problem**(?):

Often organizations focus on solving an issue and as a result new issues/problems surface to address.

This "reality" is referred to as **"The Law Of Unintended Consequences"**

Useful Tools: Monitoring and Measuring, Basic Descriptive Charts, Specifications, Control Charts and Statistical Process Control.

Phase IV: Apply and Measure
Output Summary

Use this space to record your monitoring and measurement plan for
Phase IV: Apply and Measure

Check whether you have satisfied the **EXIT** criteria for this phase:

____ 1. All relevant individuals and groups are informed of your solution and committed to supporting it.

____ 2. The plan for change is fully executed.

____ 3. Indicators are checked regularly to determine how much improvement has occurred and to spot any new problems.

Be prepared for the possibility of having your team, or team leader, make a presentation on your team's monitoring and measuring phase to your organization's leadership team. This process allows for direct communication with your leaders in order to clarify and evaluate both the solution for the problem and the effectiveness of the execution.

Steps #9 & 10: (Phase V: Success and Beyond) Standardization

Phase V Team Process

Phase V deals with the end phase of the problem identification and problem solving cycle: Success and Beyond. During this phase, you will be involved with formalizing your solution in order to establish a process owner who will be responsible for "holding the gains." This is necessary in order to keep the improvement from reverting back to the pre-improvement situation.

Suggested Steps and Guidelines...

"Maintain The Improvement"

1. Build on Success
Continuing to build both individual and group support which has been nurtured during the Results (Apply and Measure) Phase of the process, is equally as important during the Standardization (Success and Beyond) Phase. This is the time when you may train Associates on the revised process and/or standards in order to standardize the improvement throughout the organization.

2. Continue the Journey
With the idea of continuous improvement in mind, it is important that a record be kept of any significant individuals or groups which play a crucial role in continuing the success of the improvement.

3. Result of Phase V: Hold the Gains-Verification of the Improvement Effectiveness
-Has the chronic area of waste been eliminated?

-Have we checked for any new problems which may have been created by the solution?

-Have we established process ownership among appropriate staff and/or departments?

Phase V: Output Summary

4. Phase V: Output Summary A check point or milestone which determines exit criteria, results or outputs.

a. ___ All relevant individuals and groups are informed of their role in ensuring continued success with the improvement.
b. ___ Process ownership has been clarified among appropriate staff and/or departments.
c. ___ Indicators are checked regularly, by process owners to hold the gains.

5. Phase V: Communication and Feedback Process owners understand their responsibility to periodically communicate with the leadership team in order to continue the

---

Step #10: Repeat Process for Next Output, Customer or Problem

Question to Be Answered: Has a Team Presentation been made via IDEAS Storyboard to the Leadership Team?

Output Needed For Next Step: Development of future plans and celebration of team success (recognition).

See Step #1 for path forward on your Business Process Improvement Journey

Phase V: Success and Beyond
Build on Support & Continue the Journey

Use this page to keep track of key individuals or groups you have gained commitment from during Phase V. Record any significant individuals or groups which play a crucial role in continuing the success of the improvement.

Individuals or Groups Involved	Role?	Remarks

Useful Tools: Building Individual Support, Presentation

Phase V: Success and Beyond
Output Summary

Use this space to record your plan for building on success and continuing the journey during Phase V: Success and Beyond

Check whether you have satisfied the **EXIT** criteria for this phase:

____ 1. All relevant individuals and groups are informed of their role in ensuring continue success with the improvement.

____ 2. Process ownership has been clarified among appropriate staff and/or departments.

____ 3. Indicators are checked regularly, by process owners to hold the gains.

____ 4. Process owners understand their responsibility to periodically communicate with the leadership team to continue the journey.

Be prepared for the possibility of having your team, or team leader, make a presentation on your team's formalizing of the solution to your organization's leadership team. This process allows for direct communication with your leaders in order to clarify who has the responsibility to hold the gains for the improvement.

www.danduffyauthor.com
©Copyright 2019

I.D.E.A.S.: A Problem Identification and Problem Solving Process

Phase I: Identify Opportunities --CURRENT SITUATION
1. Generate and Prioritize Opportunities-**Brainstorm**
2. Select Opportunities-**Multivote**
3. Select One Problem-**Selection Grid**
4. Verify Problem-**Impact Analysis**

RESULT: Identify and Select Problem-**Problem Statement**

Output Summary: Presentation to Leadership/Management

Phase II: Determine Influential Factors--ANALYSIS
1. Decide what you need to know-**Checklist**
2. Collect Data: Baselines/Patterns-**Data Gathering**
   *** Sampling, *Survey, *Checksheet**
3. Define Critical Parameters-**Pareto-Fishbone-Flowchart** RESULT: Analyze Problem and I.D. Root Cause-**Problem Analysis**

Output Summary: Presentation to Leadership/Management

Phase III: Evaluate Alternatives--COUNTERMEASURES
1. Generate Promising Solutions-**Innovation Transfer**
2. Select One Solution-**Cost-Benefit Analysis**
3. Develop an Implementation Plan-**Force-Field Analysis**
   *** Standard Operating Procedure (SOP), *Action Plan**

RESULT: Implement Solution-**Solution for Problem & Implementation Plan**

Output Summary: Presentation to Leadership/Management

Phase IV: Apply and Measure--RESULTS
1. Gain Commitment-**Building Individual Support, Presentation**
2. Execute the Plan-**Action Plan**
3. Monitor the Impact-**Monitoring and Measuring** (before/after)
4. Measure the Results-**Monitoring and Measuring** (before/after)
   *** Basic Descriptive Charts, *Specifications and Control Limits**

RESULT: Evaluate Solution-**Gathering Support and Monitoring Situation**

Output Summary: Presentation to Leadership/Management

Phase V: Success and Beyond—STANDARDIZATION
1. Build on Success-**Building Individual Support**
2. **Train Associates on Revised Process and/or Standards**
3. Continue The Journey-**Presentation to Leadership/Management**

RESULT: Hold the Gains-**Formalizing Support and Establishing Process Ownership**

Printed in Great Britain
by Amazon